T0381202

There is no tool for development more effective than the empowerment of women

– Kofi Annan

Who Says It's A Man's World

Ageless Lessons for Becoming An Exceptional Woman

Volume I

ABIOLA "CHAMP" SALAMI

AuthorHouse™
1663 Liberty Drive
Bloomington, IN 47403
www.authorhouse.com
Phone: 1 (800) 839-8640

Published by AuthorHouse 10/05/2015

ISBN: 978-1-5049-2888-5 (sc)
ISBN: 978-1-5049-2923-3 (e)

Library of Congress Control Number: 2015916350

Print information available on the last page.

Any people depicted in stock imagery provided by Thinkstock are models,
and such images are being used for illustrative purposes only.
Certain stock imagery © Thinkstock.

This book is printed on acid-free paper.

Because of the dynamic nature of the Internet, any web addresses or links contained in this book may have changed
since publication and may no longer be valid. The views expressed in this work are solely those of the author and do not
necessarily reflect the views of the publisher, and the publisher hereby disclaims any responsibility for them.

Contents

Dedication

To Dr Ameyo Stella Shade Adadevoh, who gave the world an insight into what it means to be an exceptional woman- standing against the proliferation of an epidemic by paying the ultimate price any human can pay to save humanity.

To my Mother, the very first exceptional woman I met over 3 decades ago.

To all the exceptional exemplary women who have pioneered and promoted the course of empowering women everywhere.

To all organizations who are genuinely committed to the service of women empowerment and nourishment.

To the young girls - the women of tomorrow - who desire to be exceptional women.

Appreciation

For about 3 years, I have worked with a team of amazing people. Their selfless support and wise counsel has helped us in iamaCHAMP Limited to interpret our vision in a more strategic way and to implement this vision in a more dynamic way.

First, a big "Thank You" to my Mother - the first exceptional woman I met in my life. Thank you for the great sacrifice of allowing me to be of service to the world. Also, a big thank you to my siblings, Yetunde & Bayo Akinbogun; Olumide, Olusola & Omobolanle. Thank you for your support. To Precious, Ireoluwa & Michael, you guys are the sweetest blessing to our family.

I will like to thank Mrs. Uchenna Erobu, Mrs Laila St. Matthew Daniels, Mrs. Mavi Isibor and Hon. Abike Dabiri-Erewa for believing in me and committing to joining our first ever attempt in inspiring women at the Senior Professional Ladies' Colloquium 2013. The seed you sowed laid the foundation for this book and several other testimonies women have shared at our programs.

Also, I will like to appreciate the following exceptional women who we have been privileged to recognize, appreciate and honor for being an inspiration to young and top women through our Women Making A Difference Awards. They are: Distinguished Senator Oluremi Tinubu, Hon. Abike Dabiri-Erewa, Iyaafin Grace Titi Laoye Tomori, Prof. Remi Sonaiya, Mrs. Mo Abudu, Mrs. Uchenna Erobu and Mrs Amina Oyagbola. It is our hope that womanhood will continue to receive inspiration from you.

Also, special appreciation goes to Justice Amina Augie, Mrs. Adenike Ogunlesi, Mrs. Folasade Adefisayo, Mrs. Neka Udezue and Hon. Omobolanle Akinyemiobe for supporting us at the

CHAMP International Women's Conference.

To the wonderful young women who we have also been privileged to recognize, appreciate and honor; Adesewa Josh, Debola Deji-Kurunmi, Kemi Ajumobi, Maureen Iyasele, Rita Ezenwa-Okoro and Tolulope Otunoluwa; thank you for being an inspiration to young women in our world. I am so glad to see your commitment to passionately making a positive difference. Thank you very much for your support.

Very special thanks to my friends Kayode Ishola, Yomi Iwajomo, Wunmi Adeagbo and Gbenga Abejirin whose tireless and sacrificial efforts have helped seen the dream grow in leaps and bounds.

Also, very special thanks to Ihotu Amuta, Rhoda Robinson, Amanda Nduka, Adewunmi Oshodi Tapa and Christiana Ekpo for your contribution to making this book available. Thank you for your contributions.

Very special appreciation to Dr. Adesina Fagbenro-Byron, Mrs. Margaret Fagboyo and the British Government's Department For International Development (DFID) for your commitment to empowering women and promoting socio-economic inclusion in our country. I deeply appreciate your support towards our programs.

Also, very special appreciation to Mr. Ayo Durodola, Ms Uche Bene, Mr. Clemson Aiyegbusi, Mr. Aliyu Mohammed, Rhonda Watson, Dehab Ghebreab and the entire United States Mission for giving me the opportunity to broaden my horizon through the International Visitors Leadership Program where I met leaders doing amazing work in over 20 countries.

Very special thanks to Mr. Aigboje Aig-Imoukhuede and Dr. Herbert Wigwe for teaching me leadership, courage and tenacity; I will always appreciate the opportunity you gave me to learn and grow in Access Bank Plc. Thank you for your selfless support of our programs.

To Mr. John Obaro, I deeply appreciate your fatherly care, your personal commitment to my success since the time I worked with you till now; and your selfless support of our programs. God bless you Sir.

To Mr. Feyijimi Awosika, thank you for accepting me as your Boy, for supporting me whenever I call, for taking time to teach me valuable life-lessons. God keep you Sir.

Also, I will like to deeply appreciate Prof. Pat Utomi for all the support and lessons I have enjoyed from you over the years. God bless you Sir.

To Mr. Ken Ike Okere, thank you for being a very supporting big brother. May you never lack help in life.

To Sir Ademola Aladekomo, Mr. Jimi Agbaje and Mr. Foluso Phillps, thank you for sharing your personal time with me and your knowledge with me; we cannot forget your selfless contributions to the GAME Conferences. God bless you.

To Chief Oyekunle Alex-Duduyemi, you have been an incredible pillar of support from the very beginning and a father I'm privileged to have. I pray God will keep you in sound health and bless all your children. Thank you very much Sir.

Finally, very special appreciation to Dr. Christopher Kolade for adopting me as his son at a very crucial time when I needed the love, care and direction that only a father can give. Thank you for been a great source of inspiration Sir.

Foreword

Growing up as a girl, I saw many women live beneath their potential. I also saw a few women who were stamping their footprints and making a difference in their various endeavours, industries and sectors. Often times, the women attempting to stamp their footprints are perceived as pushy and over ambitious by those who believe a woman cannot be all that she is created to be.

While I have a lot of respect for men (as I have many of them as my contemporaries, associates, fathers and brothers, who have inspired, tutored and mentored me over the years), I do believe womanhood is a special gift from God but it has been short-changed and under-utilised for ages; and for a society to truthfully advance, we need a combination of the efforts of both men and women to reshape our world.

Abiola's realisation of this brought him to a point of contemplation where he is asking the world, 'Who Says It's A Man's World?' In my view, this question is iconic and ironic. Iconic because hardly has anyone utterly queried the statement, *It's A Man's World,* and ironic because the person querying this statement is a man himself.

It is my earnest hope that indeed, women of all ages would find in Abiola's book salient lessons needed to break barriers and transform their world. While many interventions on women empowerment appear to focus on society to provide women an opportunity, **Who Says It's a Man's World** is putting the challenge of attaining greater heights right in the palm of our hands! Abiola, by this book wants us to take personal responsibility for our success and not wait for society.

The book reminds us to be comfortable in our skins; to cultivate healthy confidence levels; manage our emotions better; provide a shoulder for other women, especially younger women; while we also make our competence too relevant to be ignored with the kind of results we achieve in everything we venture into.

Regardless of age, religion, location, culture or race, it must be our hope that womanhood - God's special gift to humanity - will be fully maximised as women everywhere accept the challenge of making a remarkable difference with their lives. No better first step in this journey than by reading this book and receiving the inspiration that Abiola has decided to share with women everywhere.

Dr. Mo Abudu

Introduction

Women come in two different kinds.

Not dark skinned or light skinned because outer colour doesn't depict inner strength; not the beautiful or the ugly because beauty is in the eyes of the beholder; not the wise or the foolish because every human on earth has made a combination of foolish and wise decisions before; not the high maintenance or the low maintenance because they are very subjective classifications of desirable standards of living; not those who want power in the world and those who want power in bed because it is a very insulting way of limiting the limitless influence of womanhood; not the goddesses and the doormats because when a woman is empowered she can become far more successful than is imaginable.

The two kinds of women are the "exceptional woman" and "soon-to-be exceptional woman".

In my opinion, trying to be a man is a total waste of *femininity*. They say *"it's a man's world"*; I am certain this statement was developed and deployed as a strategy to keep women away from industry, governance and other notable ventures in historical times. But let us consider the following for a moment;

Who says it's a man's world when there are women everywhere reshaping the world, fighting injustice, promoting peace and progress in our ill-fated world.

Who says it's a man's world when there are women leading corporations, redefining professionalism and outshining competition.

Who says it's a man's world when there are women creating change in industries and nations and continents.

Who says it's a man's world when there are women birthing and nurturing innovation in spite of human and environmental challenges.

Who says it's a man's world when there are women committed to grooming future leaders even when they don't have the support of their male partners.

Who says it's a man's world when the womanhood has the power to renew, restore and refresh.

This is why I celebrate *womanhood*!

Clearly, women are the largest untapped reservoir of talent in the world, it is my hope that this book will be read with an open mind and appropriately applied as you become the exceptional woman you have the potential of becoming.

It should however be clear to all women, exceptional or soon-to-be exceptional that this book is an attempt to espouse some ageless lessons that have carried womanhood for decades and centuries. No matter your level, these ageless lessons will help you keep living everyday like a champion regardless of whatever or whoever stands as an obstacle to your undeniable greatness.

This book is the first of many to come in this series on inspiring women. It is my desire to see more women claiming their stake in the 21st century and beyond.

Abiola "Champ" Salami

Be Comfortable In Your Skin

(Love yourself first and everything else falls in line. You really have to love yourself to get anything done in this world.)

- Lucille Ball

From my observation over the years, women with good self-esteem advance towards becoming exceptional far more than women who have low self-esteem and it is all in the mind. You can't have a mindset that you are not beautiful and expect people to think you are beautiful. No matter how articulate their positive words may be, you will always listen with your mind not your ears.

Beauty is how you feel inside, and it reflects in your eyes. It is not something physical. That is why nobody can make you feel inferior without your consent. No matter what society says or what your friends say, it should not keep you down. Most times, the world is unfair and this state of the social cosmos should not form the basis of your personal perception.

Without your permission, the world has become a mirror reflecting its own definition of beauty, success and who a woman should be.

Perhaps you were told your face was oily; so you start using oil control skin care cosmetics. The cosmetics work fine but you still feel inadequate because the world sold an idea to you that made you less comfortable in your skin.

Perhaps you were told, you are short; so you start wearing high heel shoes and you expected to feel tall and rock those shoes like the tall you, but despite wearing those high heels, you still feel short and inadequate because the world sold an idea to you that made you less comfortable in your skin.

Perhaps you were told that you are too black and not sexy enough; so you start using different pills and cosmetics to make your skin look finer and doing many things to get your sexy on. Even though you look better now, you still don't feel better because the world sold an idea to you that still makes you less comfortable in your skin.

If you desire to become an exceptional woman, you need to look in the right direction for getting your self-approval. You need to check what your mirror is reflecting and what that reflection is feeding your mind. Some women use their friends as their mirrors, but when you use jealous friends as mirrors, you can only

On a regular basis, look into your mirror and hug yourself. Tell yourself: "Hello, My Pretty Exceptional Angel ! You are too precious to the world" expect to see them reflect jealousy and when they reflect jealousy, they feed your mind with their opinions which is seldom to strengthen you.

Some young ladies are so starved for male approval that what should be normal attraction to men is accelerated into an obsessive need for male affirmation. The tragedy is, these precious, potentially exceptional women allow themselves to be abused in the arms of men who neither regard nor respect them as human beings.

There is no better time for women to start seeing their beauty from inside-out, there is no better time for women to start seeing their strength from inside-out. If you use a mirror, that mirror must reflect what you have inside you.

Any mirror around you that makes you feel less confident about yourself or makes you feel less beautiful or makes you feel less powerless should be changed. If the mirror in your house tells you that you are not beautiful, you need to get a new mirror. Why? That mirror must be wrong. You need to change from the mirror that reflects your limitations to the one that esteems your limitless influence.

You may be thinking, *Abiola! Let's get real.* But, What is real to you? Is it real that you were created to be ugly? I say No! Were you created to get a definition of yourself from any man or woman? I say No! Were you created to be at the mercy of another person? I dare say No!

Rather, you were created as a perfect, beautiful woman. You may not be Miss World but you are the miss of your world. You might not have been called the most beautiful girl in your immediate environment but you are the most beautiful girl of your own environment.

As much as a facelift is a good way to have your dream look, facelifts do not repair the dent the world has made on your self-esteem. You can pump it up, you can tuck it and remodel it but if it is not from inside you, your encasement will be beautiful but your inner being will remain frustrated. Your mirror will tell you, you are looking good but your eyes will tell you different.

There is nothing more terrible than a frustrated beautiful woman - a woman with a broken spirit, shattered self-esteem & negative self-concept. A woman whose heart of gold has been devalued by her attempt to fit in, whose originality has been devoured by emotional trauma, whose self-concept has been slaughtered by the opinions and biases and prejudices of the world around her.

A woman, who has given her all, made the sacrifices and tried all she could to hold the marriage together but the marriage fell flat and she has not been able to hold herself together. She gave her all, tried her best possible to keep herself from assault and abuse but she got abused and she still constantly gets abused and abuse for her, is now the norm. She gave her all to raise her kids to become the best children within and beyond the neighbourhood but the more she taught them, the farther they get from her motherhood care and wisdom. She sees herself in her little girl and tries to lead the little not to end up like her but her little girl's notoriety degenerating in a geometric regression.

While all these issues are true and real, they should not impact your esteem. There are things you can control and there are others you can't. The wisdom here is having the calmness to recognize the things you cannot change, the audacity to change the things you can and the good judgment to know the difference. No matter what happens to you, don't lose your esteem.

Your esteem is the source of your power. Whatever depletes your esteem depletes your power; avoid them. Whatever improves your esteem increases your power; allow them. Your esteem gives fire to your passion. Whatever can kindle your fire can kill your exceptional nature, avoid them. Whatever gets you inspired, re-energised and refilled will move you faster towards becoming an exceptional woman.

You are probably asking, so how do I remain comfortable in my skin? It is by doing two things everyday: *watching the words to your world & watching the words from your world.*

In her book, *The Thirteenth Tale*, Diane Setterfield said "*there is something about words. In expert hands, manipulated deftly, they take you prisoner. Wind themselves around your limbs like spider silk, and when you are so enthralled you cannot move, they pierce your skin, enter your blood, numb your thoughts. Inside you they work their magic*". That is exactly how words work.

Words have the capacity to break or make every woman. Womanhood is neither exonerated from the evident consequence of the words spoken to her nor the words she speaks to herself. The *words to your world* are the words you speak to yourself and about yourself while the *words from your world* are those people speak about you-directly or indirectly.

Some women self-destruct by sending negative words into their world. When you see a woman who talks herself down, who sees herself as a victim of her circumstances, who use *pity-words* to describe herself, who blames everyone and everything for her undesirable state, that woman unconsciously dis-empowers herself. This is not about living in self-denial; rather it is about getting in the driver's seat of your life with your word-power. Woman, your words are powerful because they give action to your thoughts; your words are powerful because the limit of your language is the limit of your power.

More than any creature, there exists for all women a narrative – a series of words that have the power to destroy the power of womanhood. Another narrative exists, another series of words that could heal you. If you're lucky you will get the second, but you can be certain of getting the first. It is your duty to position yourself towards benefitting from the largesse of the words that could heal you.

Whether it is about building your esteem, or about your interaction with others, especially other women, *words are like eggs dropped from great heights; you can no more call them back than ignore the mess they leave when they fall.*

It's okay to cry especially when you are overwhelmed. Crying doesn't mean you are weak, it means you are human. When you cry therefore; wipe your own tears, pick yourself up, look into the mirror, hold yourself tight and say to yourself "Darling, You Are Bigger than this situation "

While you don't have control over what anybody says about you, you have the power to control your reaction to what people say about you.

You need to have the *'Let them say'* attitude. In your industry, your family and your community, there are envious and jealous people everywhere around you.

Jealous and envious people who wished they had what you have, and because they don't, they want you to think you have nothing so that they can steal what you have   or at worst ensure you never have it again and neither do they.

Their jealousy and envy leads them to communicate erroneous opinions about you. They could tell the world that you are too proud because you are more beautiful, more successful or more blissful. They will say *'you too dey do'*. They will say *'your own is too much'*. They will say *'But you are just a woman'*. They will talk you down and say you can't be great. They could say you are good for nothing.

Life could be so challenging when you have people like this all around you. You get more disappointed when you realise that those saying negative things about you are supposed to be your closest allies - folks you've always trusted, always sacrificed for and always cared for. This could be quite frustrating but what you should always know is that everyone has a right to their opinion but you have a right to your decision.

The opinion of another person should NOT become your reality. If they say you are too short or too tall or too black or too fair or too fat or too skinny or too emotional or too rigid, You have the authority to look them in the eye and say these five powerful words; *I am perfect as I am.*

You need to be comfortable in your skin; else the world will give

While you don't have control over what anybody says about you, you have the power to control your reaction to what people say about you.

The first step to cultivating healthy self-esteem is to love yourself first; any other love can then follow.

you too much trouble that you may get frustrated, depressed and suicidal. The #1 cause of suicide according to Psychology Today is Severe Depression.

Although psychologists recommend that if you suspects someone might be depressed, don't allow your tendency to deny the possibility of contemplating suicide prevent you from asking about it BUT mean people with their envious, jealous and callous opinion, will lead you faster to suicide that Hussein Bolt will complete a 4X400m dash.

I have news for you - good news and bad news. I won't bother asking you, because I guess most people want to hear the bad news first. So, the bad news is you cannot totally avoid people who will speak negative *words from your world*, but the good news is you can resist the impact of their words on your world by constantly stuffing yourself with words that empower you, fires you up and improves your esteem.

Confessions are a great way of helping you remain confident, powerful and comfortable in your skin. Take them seriously and conscientiously. The following excerpt will surely help build your internal power.

Confession

I am more than just an option, I am exceptional
I am more than just a number, I am number 1 ordinary
I am more than just statistic in the world; I am a significant influence in my world the world I am more than one strong being; I am beautiful, bold and the best all in one package
I am more than beautiful; I am precious, gorgeous and luxurious,
I am more than precious; I am ageless, boundless, ceaseless, doubtless, endless & fearless
I am more than fearless; I am full of wisdom, knowledge and understanding
I am more than a sweet lover; I am a dependable builder, a caring cultivator and a strong fortress
I bring more than a smile to my world; I brighten up everywhere I go and everyone I meet

Be Confident

Confidence is the sexiest thing any woman can ever wear; self doubt is the deadliest thing any woman can ever have .

Women have always been powerful. So powerful that even in situations where male heroes bowed their heads in surrender, women stood up to avenge and conquer. However, many women have taken the 'erroneous weaker vessel opinion' proposing that women are the weaker gender.

If you doubt your ability to accomplish something, then you can't accomplish it. You need to have confidence in your ability, and then be strong enough to follow through.

From historical times to contemporary time, when we consider what women have achieved in bringing peace to the world, in leading industries, nurturing human species, in birthing innovation and several other first-rate achievements, we will see that the weaker vessel concept many hold is erroneous. Please know that you may look like a breakable, frail, fragile glass outside but you are a strong solid rock on the inside. Because I believe you can do very extraordinary things.

A woman is a steel inside but velvet outside. She could be gentle but also severe and firm. The weaker vessel concept is erroneous because it gives the world - men and women alike - the notion of velvet and not steel. Women were created to have incomparable inner strength and it is important you understand this, appreciate it and carry on confidently in all that you do. Always know that you can do more than what you think you can do.

A 2004 study of Harvard Law School classrooms found that men were 50 percent more likely than women to volunteer at least one comment during class, and 144 percent more likely to speak voluntarily at least three times. While some writers have blamed this outcome on men and on the culture, history is filled with examples of women whose courageous acts can inspire women to be more confident.

believe you can and you're halfway there.

The Trung Sisters

In Vietnam, women have always been in the forefront in resisting foreign domination. Two of the most popular heroines are the Trung sisters who led the first national uprising against the Chinese, who had previously conquered them in the year 40 A.D. The Vietnamese had been suffering under the harsh rule of a Chinese governor called To Dinh. Some feel that if the sisters had not resisted the Chinese when they did, there would be no Vietnamese nation today.

The sisters were daughters of a powerful lord. Trung Trac was the elder; Turng Nhi, her constant companion, the younger. They lived in a time when Vietnamese women enjoyed freedoms forbidden them in later centuries. For example, women could not inherit property through their mother's line and become political leaders, judges, traders and warriors.

Trung Trac was married to Thi Sach, another powerful lord. Chinese records note that Trac had a "brave and fearless disposition". It was she who mobilised the Vietnamese lords to rebel against the Chinese. Legend syas that to gain the confidence of the people, the Trung sisters committed acts of bravery, such as killing a fearful people-eater tiger- and used the tiger's skin as paper to write a proclamation urging the people to follow them against the Chinese.

The Trungs gathered an army of 80,000 people to help drive the Chinese from their lands. From among those who came forward to fight the Chinese, the Trung sisters chose thirty-six women, including their mother. They trained them to be generals. Many names of the leaders of the uprising recorded in temples dedicated To Trung Trac are women. These women led a people's army of 80,000 which drove the Chinese out of Viet Nam in 40 A.D. The Trung Sisters, of whom Hni proved to be the better warrior, liberated six-five fortresses.

After their victory, the people proclaimed Trung Trac to be their ruler. They renamed her "Trung Vuong" or "She-king Trung". She established her royal court in Me-linh, an acient political center in the Hong River plain. As queen, she abolished the hated tribute taxes which had been imposed by the Chinese. She also attempted to restore a simpler form of government more in line with traditional Vietnamese values.

The story of The Trung Sisters is a source of pride for womanhood; it is a patriotic display of heroism and a testament to the fact that you have the *power to do more than you think you can do.*

While your vocation may not literally involve you taking up arms and ammunitions to fight against foreign domination and aggression, there are perhaps issues that pose as foreign domination and aggression in your career, family, marriage, friendships and communities which you have the power to correct.

In certain workplaces, there is a notion (a very annoying notion) that "it's either a woman has good body or good brain; good brain and good body together is very hard to find". This statement is annoying because many men and women alike think and act in line with the statement. Men objectify women and women too objectify women.

Isn't it demeaning that a man tells you as his professional subordinate to help pick up something because he wants to check out your behind? Isn't it demeaning that you get into a formal meeting to gain attention with your fascinating frontal features? Now, you know what to expect but you carry on, trying to make up for inadequate competence or confidence.

Your confidence should emanate from the conviction that you can deliver excellence far beyond your expectation; your confidence should emanate from an understanding that you are the finished product of creation (i.e. the final creature God created). Your confidence should grow from the ever-true knowledge that because you are the final work of God's creation, your spirit, soul and body was designed and equipped to be the best of creation.

I am jealous of women. And again I say, I am jealous of women. I am jealous of women because women are the final work of God's creation whose spirit, soul and body was designed and equipped to be the best of all creation. Sadly, many women (old & young) don't realise their strength, finesse and uniqueness. Hence, some women feel powerless, wallowing in the murky waters of low self-esteem — many asking men for "Women's Rights". Why ask another creature for power and permission to do what you have already been empowered and commissioned to do since creation. This is why I am sad. I am sad and I am committed to supporting every woman — young and old - to discover she is a champion; to discover she can become a phenomenal woman and help her became the exceptional woman she was meant to be.

The Trung Sisters in our story saw beyond their facial beauty, they saw beyond their fascinating frontal features, they saw beyond their admirable backside and they saw beyond their royalty. They saw themselves as women who could make a difference in their nation. Women who when even all the male heroes bowed their heads in submission to the foreign aggression of China; they proudly stood up to avenge the country.

SELF CONFIDENCE

You can't live your exceptional life without it; You can't manage your exceptional status without it; You can't make sterling progress without it.

Opinions & Self Confidence

Everyone has a right to their opinion, but you have a right to your decision. Almost every opinion around a woman is fighting her to reduce her confidence level to the barest minimum and there seem to be nothing helping to boost this confidence.

The Entertainment industry through her Siamese twin - the Media - keeps objectifying the physiological endowment of a woman as though that is all about a woman; and if you don't have what is physiologically acceptable, it impacts your self esteem negatively. This is why many women forcefully comply with a fad; their confidence is from the media opinion about what is in vogue. Yes, it is good to be trendy but your confidence should not be media or entertainment laden; your confidence should come from inside of you.

While I agree that womanhood is one of the finest expressions of God's ultimate creativity, I believe more that womanhood is the best of God's ultimate reservoir that is largely untapped. Women are the largest untapped reservoir of talent in the world.

The world is afraid of this untapped reservoir so they confuse women with the weaker vessel concept, such that when a woman buys this opinion, she becomes disempowered and sees herself less than she actually is and believes in her ability less than she actually can.

The world is afraid of this narrative so they dominate womanhood in every facet of livelihood. She is dominated in the workplace, dominated in marriage, dominated in the community, dominated in political leadership with cultural explanations for the domination.

The world is afraid of this untapped reservoir so they deceive women by accentuating and worshipping the fascinating, admirable, charming and delectable velvet woman body through entertainment without making any attempt to initiate a conversation about the true power of women which lies on the inside.

This narrative has to change! Not tomorrow, not next week, not next month, not next year, not next decade but now. We need to start giving the same level of attention we have given to the physiology of womanhood to the potential of womanhood.

The first step to this my dear woman is, believe in yourself so strongly that the world can't help but believe in you too such that you shock the world with your achievements in every responsibility you have.

One woman whose confidence I admire is Chimamanda Adichie. I can comfortably assume that her confidence is derived from an understanding of who she is years before she became a global icon. I once read a quote credited to her online; please read this carefully- "Of course I am not worried about intimidating men. The type of man who will be intimidated by me is exactly the type of man I have no interest in".

Confidence Confession

I am more than my body, my brain is actively productive and my mind is actively creative
I am strong and empowered; I have focus and determination, I will always stand up for myself and my beliefs
I approve of myself and love myself deeply and completely; I am outgoing and confident in social situations
Every breathe into my nostril inhales confidence and every breathe out of my nostril exhales timidity
I am energetic and enthusiastic and I have unbreakable confidence within myself I decide and take action
I am transformed into someone who always stands up for what I believe in
I am not a princess that needs to be saved by a prince; I am a queen that is an asset to a king.

Believe in yourself so strongly that the world can't help but believe in you; such that you shock the world with your outstanding achievements in every responsibility you have.

Be The #1 Lifter of Other Women

A flower does not think of competing with the flower next to it. It just blooms.

- Zen Shin

Halima was an admirable, beautiful and delectable lady whose mother was the envy of all women because of Halima's level of intelligence, her fast-paced career and her decorum. Uche was Halima's childhood friend and they share lots of fond memories together. Halima & Uche attended the same primary, secondary and tertiary schools. Both ladies were intelligent and everyone that knew them together thought they were twins because of the resemblance they shared, not physiologically but in their positive attitude, their strong bond and the excellent results both ladies achieved all through their school days.

In their Secondary School days, there were many episodes of Halima and Uche sleeping over in each other's houses and their parents had no reason to panic because they trust whenever they don't find one of them, she must definitely be in the other's house. Of course by the time they were writing entrance examination into University, both of them planned to attend the same school, stay in the same dormitory but they were to study different but very similar courses – Electrical Engineering and Civil Engineering.

Halima and Uche lived together, gossiped together, read together, loved each other and fought for each other. On a particular occasion, 6 girls accused Halima of stealing the makeup kit belonging to one of them. Without listening to anybody's explanation, Uche tore down the roof in defence of Halima. Uche changed the story, accusing the 6 girls of stealing, jealousy and attempted battery. Uche and Halima graduated from the University on top of their set, not just their class.

After school, Halima got a job immediately with one of the first generation banks as a Client Service Officer managing the accounts of High Net-worth Individuals. From an average Lagos girl, Halima started mingling with the crème de la crème in the society. You would find Halima in high class events with pictures on the popular blogs & newspapers. Within few months, Halima became a force to be reckoned with at her bank and in the Lagos metropolis. Despite her exposure and level of success, Halima was still very polite and humble.

While life was bubbling for Halima, life was not budding for Uche who was yet to get a meaningful job 18 months after graduating with a good class of degree. By this time, many would have lost hope especially seeing her friend balling with a career on the fast track but Uche remained resolute. Although she could not afford Brazilian, Peruvian or German hair, she still remained firm in her conviction of landing a great job soon. Although she could not afford to buy a car, she could rent a cab from her meagre salary when she had important outings. Uche understood that *if you whine while waiting, you may wither; but if you work while waiting, you will win.* Both ladies were still very good friends none envious, jealous or malicious of the other.

At exactly 24 months after graduation, Uche got a fantastic job in the oil industry. The Chairman of the company was one of Halima's clients who Halima has been persuading for about 9 months to get her friend on board. Halima had also switched to that company with a mouth-watering offer as a Manager, 3 months before Uche joined. With the structure of the organisation, Uche had a new boss – her childhood friend. Uche got married 6 months after getting the job. Halima, despite her economic and social status was still very single as most of the guys who are interested in her were at the same time intimidated by her success, despite her cool and calm nature. Halima got comfort from the words of Chimamanda Adichie *"Of course I am not worried about intimidating men. The type of man who will be intimidated by me is exactly the type of man I have no interest in"*. Halima held on, persisted, kept improving on herself, didn't allow her singlehood to become loneliness, she spent her single time, preparing for her marriage and family in a very responsible way.

Despite Uche's marital success, she always encouraged Halima. She recommended potential hubby to Halima. She prayed for Halima. Anytime Halima's parents mount pressure on their daughter, Uche was there to undo the pressure. Anytime Halima is fearful about her age, single status, menopause and delayed marriage, Uche was always there to allay Halima's fears.

Despite how strong Halima was, there were many times she would be at the verge of falling into depression, because she could see all her friends and younger ones getting married – some of which she played significant financial roles. She saw these married couples giving birth and their children are growing and attending school but here she is without a man of her own, let alone a child of her own.

At age 41, Halima met Henry a tall, dark and handsome guy. This man was 34 and his love for Halima was so much that Halima shed tears of joy anytime Henry showered his love on her. Henry was that kind of guy who would take his time before loving but once he stepped into the love dance floor, he came bearing gifts of love. Henry was the envy of all of Halima's friends who were married.

One would have thought that at Halima's age, she wouldn't find such a handsome, young responsible man to fall head over heels in love with her. Often times, Halima will hide herself in closet and pinch herself to be sure her new lease of life was true.

Exactly nine months after Halima met Henry, they got married. Halima entered a new level in life and everything in her life started blossoming like a tree planted by the river, receiving nourishment from the earth and energy from the sunlight consistently.

Years later, Halima had forgotten the pain of waiting; she now enjoys the gain of a blissful and peaceful marriage. All thanks to Uche, who understood what it meant to be an exceptional woman. She understood that real success for an exceptional woman comes from lifting other women and comforting them in their times of need.

Rather than comforting other women, ordinary women compete with other women but that is not the case for exceptional women. It is often said that a woman's arch enemy is another woman, not a man.

Lifting and comforting women is not just about what you say to their faces, it is also what you say behind their back. It is not just about the positive actions that you put up, it is about the positive thoughts that you have about them. I believe the worst place in hell is reserved for people who will appear to lift you to your face, whereas they are pulling you down behind you.

Lifting and comforting other women means that you will be the #1 fan of every woman you encounter- on the job, in your family, in your place of worship, on the plane, anywhere and at anytime. It means you will be the first-rate, self-employed advocate of women-not with noise-making and protests but with tact, decorum and selflessness.

Lifting other women is a genuine commitment to providing a shoulder for other women by caring and showing that you care and by being a beacon of hope for women by the way you pursue, achieve and balance your career/business and domestic responsibilities. It means you have an understanding that discomfort to any woman anywhere is discomfort to every woman everywhere.

The story of Halima and Uche teaches certain lessons exceptional women should take on in adding value to womanhood. To become an exceptional woman therefore it is important that we bear the following in mind:

1. Ordinary women compete with each other; but exceptional women empower each other.

The success of any woman anywhere should inspire you to dream more, aim more and achieve more. It is only an ordinary woman who gets jealous and envious of the success of another woman. When you set out to compete, you lose focus of your own goal, you kill your potential, you weaken your unique natural strengths, you feel good but can never feel great and you miss golden opportunities to learn. Competition is limitation.

The goal is not competition, the goal is completing; the role is not competitive, the role is complementary. You can tell who the exceptional women are. They are the ones you will always find building one another up instead of tearing each other down.

2. The exceptional woman knows her worth, she doesn't measure herself against another woman but she stands strong, calm and self-confident

Even if another woman looks more beautiful, has more money, wields more power, has more fame, has a more beautiful home and a wonderful husband and you don't have one or more of these, the ordinary attitude is for you to think less of yourself. Instead, look inwards and be grateful for what you have. When you are grateful for your level of success, an ocean of positive hormone springs from inside you filling you with confidence as you aspire to acquire your desire of becoming more exceptional.

Anytime you determine how successful you are based on the success or failure of another woman, you kill your potential or increase your internal pressure. Measuring yourself against another woman leads you to competition. You don't have to compete to be outstanding; all you need is discover your purpose, grow towards your maximum potential and sow seeds to benefit others. Many women have made choices that destroyed their potentials because they consistently compare themselves with other women; because they are not grateful and thankful for what they have, they lose their originality.

An Exceptional Woman understands that real success comes from lifting other women and comforting them in their times of need.

You need to realise that your strength, no matter how little, is a natural raw material that you need to turn over to work-in-progress and then to finished goods and no matter who is achieving more.

3. The prettiest smiles hide the deepest secrets; the prettiest eyes cry the most tears and the kindest of hearts have felt the most pain.

The fact that a woman looks good and great, bright and beautiful doesn't mean she is alright. Haven't you asked someone if anything is wrong; and it is obvious from their initial expression or tone of voice that they're worried, only to have them respond: "No, I'm fine."? In such instances, clearly they're *not* fine but they feel secure retreating into themselves to avoid a dialogue they fear might end up making them feel worse. Psychologists say that women are much more likely to hide their emotional distress because they don't want to be told that they're too "thin-skinned" or more commonly, "too sensitive". Bottom line is that we should look beyond the smiles of others and show genuine concern and affection when they go through hard times. With this kind of supportive gesture, we will help *safeguard* and *validate* the vulnerability of other women.

Helping The Girls And Hindering The Boys

Halima had the responsibility of leading a team of five which consisted of Ibiwari, Akpan, Ahmed, Denike and her childhood friend, Uche. On the job, Halima observed that Denike maintained a good relationship with Ibiwari and Uche but she didn't share same with Akpan and Ahmed. While Denike speaks for Uche and Ibiwari, she speaks against Akpan and Ahmed.

On a particular occasion, Halima's team had the responsibility of organising the Annual General Meeting for the oil company. Uche was in charge of hospitality, Akpan was in charge of logistics, Ahmed was in charge of communications, Ibiwari was in charge documentation, Denike was in charge of vendors and Halima was to oversee the team.

Denike was always perturbed at Halima's approach to leadership. Denike expected Halima to support the girls and always give the boys a hard time. Often times she would say to

Halima jokingly "*Boss, cut a girl some slack*". Denike's definition of supporting women is about giving women the opportunity to shine while keeping their male counterparts from shinning. Denike believed that men have always being at the forefront and it is time for women to take over everywhere and in her world, this starts from her present job.

Denike's philosophy is that women have been abused and misused over the years by men and it is time to repay men for their wrongdoings over the past centuries and she is set to maximise every opportunity she has to carry out this vengeance. For Denike, women empowerment means men disempowerment. Her opinion is that anything that promotes women should silently demote men; to her, for every one positive action towards a woman, there should be a corresponding negative action towards a man. It's all about helping the girls and hindering the boys.

Denike expected Halima's leadership to be strategically positioned to help the girls and hinder the boys. However, Halima understood she was not a leader or advocate of either her female team members only or her male team members only or even her childhood friend - she had responsibility over all of them and to be an effective leader and an exceptional woman, she needs to lead and advocate for her team as one united entity regardless of gender or personal relationship.

Halima understood that you cannot fix yourself by breaking someone else. She also understood that you don't fight injustice with injustice; you don't fight unfair treatment with unfair treatment. Rather than leave Denike to her thoughts, Halima decided to coach Denike on how to be pro-woman and not anti-man at the same time.

Who are the Exceptional Women? They are those who care for others regardless of age, gender, race, color or socio-economic status.

Confession: Pledge of Support

I commit to supporting every woman I come in contact with anywhere in the world

I commit to using my words and my deeds to promote others – women and men alike

My commitment is to be a better person today than I was yesterday; and to be a better person tomorrow than I am today.

I pledge to be kind to other women and men regardless of my past experience

I pledge to be grateful for what I have, hopeful for a better tomorrow and faithful in developing my ability as an exceptional woman

From where I am now, I pledge to provide material and non-material support to every woman in need to the best of my ability

As I achieve more feats in life, I pledge to mentor more women, support more women and sponsor more women to become exceptional

As I admire the achievements of other exceptional women, I get inspired by it and I get motivated to be exceptional

Happy Women's Day

My Women's Day 2015 Message

Whether you are a girl just getting into the world today, a young lady in school, a professional upwardly mobile lady or a senior lady in the class of a mother, grandmother or great grandmother; anywhere you are in the world, here is wishing you Happy Women's Day.

I have three emotions for women: 1) I LOVE women 2) I am JEALOUS of women 3) I am SAD about womanhood.

For me, a woman isn't just that human creature who's got a fine face, fascinating frontal features & an admirable backside. No! No!! No!!! No!!!! For me, a woman is the finished product of creation; a woman is the complete creature created by the Creator. This is why I love women.

Because she's the complete creature created by the Creator, her spirit, soul & body was designed & equipped to be the best of creation. This is why I am jealous of women.

However, many women don't realise their strength, finesse & uniqueness; so, they feel powerless, wallowing in the murky waters of low self-esteem - many asking men for 'Women's Right' because of the erroneous belief that it's a man's world. A man's world? This is why I am sad.

My Dear Woman, please consider the following for a while:

Who says it's a man's world when there are women everywhere reshaping the world, fighting injustice, promoting peace and progress in our ill-fated world;

Who says it's a man's world when there are women leading corporations, redefining professionalism and outshining competition;

Who says it's a man's world when there are women creating change in industries and nations and continents;

Who says it's a man's world when there are women birthing and nurturing innovation in spite of human and environmental difficulties;

Who says it's a man's world when there are women committed to grooming future leaders even when they don't have the support of their male partners;

Who says it's a man's world when womanhood has the power to renew, restore and refresh.

Who says it's a man's world leaving you asking another creature for power & permission to do what you have already being empowered & commissioned to do by the Creator.

My Dear Woman, please don't focus on man for your empowerment, success & progress.

This is not an excuse for dehumanizing, disrespecting or disregarding men; as we need the contributions of both men and women to create a better world. Rather, it's a call for womanhood to look inwards, acquire knowledge, believe in yourself, understand & deliver on your role in your society.

And to the men, this occasion is a reminder for us to support the empowerment of womanhood.
Not by thinking women are our possessions like cars or lands or that women are our stress bags or punch bags but by understanding our role of leading, educating & encouraging all the women in our lives.

My dear woman, the Creator has already given you the right to lead by influence in the society, right to ensure continuity of society, right to use your competence & character to birth change in the society and lots more.

My Dear Woman, if no one else loves you, know that I love you; if no one else believes in you, I believe in you and; if no one else celebrates you today, please note that I celebrate you.

God bless every woman in the world. Happy Women's Day! My name is Abiola Salami, I Speak to Champions.

© *Abiola Salami, February 2015*

Everyday A Mother's Day

1. How can we imagine the excruciating pain and agony of carrying a foetus for 270 days

   How else would we have obtained proper nutrition at every stage of our developmental days

   How can we imagine the sacrifices and commitment from our conception to our maturation How else would we have obtained intelligence and creativity without the early touch of motherhood

   How can we appreciate her for multi-tasking, multi-feeding, multi-supporting, multi-committing and multi-stretching

2. Who else would have given us full attention, full commitment and full succour even in our adult years

   Who else would be communicating without speaking and you'll get the message succinctly so far you can read her face

   Who else would be patient with our foolishness

   Who else would be kind with our errors

   Who else would care and care again and again even when the beneficiary of the care doesn't care about her care

3. What else could be more comforting than the shield of warmth embrace from the world's #1 Bodyguard

    What else could be more assuring than the hope of healthy living as provided by the world's #1 Therapist

    What else could be more satisfying than the hope of fresh home-made meals from the world's #1 Chef

    What else could be more fulfilling than the in-built confidence from the positive words of the world's #1 Advocate

    What else could be rewarding to this #1 BodyGuard, #1 Therapist, #1 Chef and #1 Advocate than a sincere appreciation

MOTHERS, on behalf of all the CHAMPIONS you have raised, those you are raising and those you will still raise, here's is saying a big THANK YOU.

©Abiola Salami, 15.03.2015

GAME
Goal Attainment Made Easy

THEM
"Total Well-Being Goals
Repositioning, Rethinking & Re-igniting
for the Future.

29th – 30th November, 201

Radisson Blu Hotel
Victoria Island, Lago

Powered b

Senior Professional Ladies' Colloquium 2013

In 2013, we engaged about 100 women through the Senior Professional Ladies' Colloquium at Radisson Blu Hotel where women were empowered to balance their family, relationship and career demands. We hosted Hon. Abike Dabiri-Erewa, Mrs Mo Abudu, Mrs Uchenna Erobu, Mrs Laila St Matthew Daniels and Mrs Mavi Isibor. The Senior Professional Ladies' Colloquium was delivered as an integral part of the CHAMP's annual GAME Conference dubbed as Africa's #1 workforce productivity conference.

Hon. Abike Dabiri-Erewa | Mrs Uche Erobu | Mrs Laila St Matthew Daniel | Mrs Mo Abudu | Mrs Salami, Mrs Mavi Isibor, Hon. Abike Dabiri-Erewa, Mrs Uche Erobu & Abiola Salami

Cross Section of Women paying attention to the speakers

Cross Section of Women taking The Exceptional Pledge

Delegates from Fidelity Bank, Akintola WilliamsDeloitte, Lagos Business School & British High Commission contributing at the colloquium

20 TO 22 NOVEMBER 2014

GAME 2014
Goal Attainment Made Easy

Africa's #1 Conference on Workforce Productivity

Theme:
The Making of Most Valuable Players

Hon. Abike Dabiri-Erewa | Abiola Salami | Dr Alex Otti (OFR) | Dr. Christopher Kolade (CON) | Foluso Phillips | Herbert Wigwe | Jimi Agbaje (OON)

Ken Okere | Dr. Mo Abudu | Dr. Oby Ezekwesili (OFR) | Prof. Patrick Utomi | Uchenna Erobu | Yewande Sadiku | Gen. Yakubu Gowon GCFR, GCON

For enquiries:
📞 09037957970; 08055547400 **URL** www.gameafrica.org
🐦 @GameAfrica 📘 GameAfrika ✉ enquiries@gameafrica.org

Venue:
Civic Centre,
Ozumba Mbadiwe, Victoria Island, Lagos

Women Making A Difference Awards

The CHAMP Women Making A Difference Award is a recognition and appreciation for women who are making an exceptional difference with their creativity, competence, character, compassion and candor in their chosen fields. In 2014, the awards was an integral part of the CHAMP's annual GAME Conference dubbed as Africa's #1 workforce productivity conference. The program was delivered with the British Government's Department For International Development and supported by Access Bank Plc.

Sights & Scenes

(1) Dr. Adesina Fagbenro-Byron & Mrs Margaret Fagboyo of the Department of International Development (DFID) and representatives of Osun State Government

(2) Chief Mrs Adeyi, representative of Iyaafin Grace Titi Laoye-Tomori, Deputy Governor of the State of Osun

(3) Hon. Abike Dabiri-Erewa presenting an award to the Deputy Governor of the State of Osun.

(4) Maureen Iyasele for Youth Empowerment (5) Kemi Ajumobi for Women Empowerment (6) Adesewa Josh for Media Excellence

(7) Hon. Abike Dabiri-Erewa and Abiola Salami during The AbiolaChamp Show

(8) Onyeka Emenibah, receiving the award for Exemplary Professional Services on behalf of her mother, Mrs. Uchenna Erobu

(9) Hon. Abike Dabiri-Erewa receiving an award for Media Excellence & Political Leadership

(10) Representative of Access Bank Plc discussing the Access W offerings with women delegates

11) Award recipients and Special Guests at a glance

12) Some red carpet images

(13) Abiola Salami, Convener of CHAMP's Women Making A Difference Awards

International Women's Conference

Theme:
Empowering Women To Secure The Future

FACULTY

Hon. Abike Dabiri-Erewa | Abiola Salami | Cordelia Okpei | Debola Deji Kurunmi | Folasade Adefisayo

Michelle Patterson | Mrs Ogunlesi | Neka Udeze | Professor Remi Sonaiya | Yetunde Ilori

SESSIONS:
WOMEN ENTERPRENEURSHIP | MANAGING WORK & FAMILY
WOMEN IN LEADERSHIP | WOMEN MAKING A DIFFERENCE AWARDS

Venue:
Eko Hotel & Suites, Victoria Island, Lagos.

Date:
22ND AUG 2015 | 9AM

For more information visit www.abiolachamp.com

CHAMP International Women's Conference 2015

It was a great pleasure inspiring, engaging and celebrating womanhood at the maiden edition of the CHAMP International Women's Conference 2015 which was held at Eko Hotel & Suites, Victoria Island, Lagos. The conference had discussions on Women Enterprise; Career & Family Management; Women in Leadership and the grand finale was the Women Making A Difference Awards which celebrated 3 amazing women.

(1) Abiola Salami inspiring women at the opening session of CHAMP IWC2015. (2) Cross section of delegates taking the CHAMP Creed (3) Cross section of delegates taking notes (4) Cross section of delegates listening attentively to Abiola Salami (5) Mrs Adenike Ogunlesi, Panel Chair (6) Mrs Folasade Adefisayo, Panel Chair (7) Mrs Victoria Adewunmi Panelist (8) Mrs Neka Udezue, Panel Co-Chair (9) Abiola Salami responding to question (10) Cross section of delegates paying attention (11) Cross section of delegates participating (12) A delegate asking a question (13) Another delegate asking a question (14) Delegates & Faculty Photo Session (15) Delegates & Faculty Photo Session (16) Delegates & Faculty Photo Session (17) The Women Making A Difference Awards Symbol (18) Mrs Amina Oyagbola of MTN Nigeria receiving an award (19) Prof. Remi Sonaya, Nigerian Presidential Candidate 2015 receiving an award presented by the US Acting Consul General, Dehab Ghebreab (20) Hon. Omobolanle Akinyemiobe receiving the award on behalf of Distinguished Senator Oluremi Tinubu as jointly presented by the Co-ordinator DFID, Dr. Adesina Fagbenro-Byron and US Acting Consul General, Dehab Ghebreab (21) The VIPs and Award recipients from left: Ms Dehab Ghebreab, Acting Consul General, US Consulate; Mr. Abiola Salami, Chief Executive iamaCHAMP Limited; representative of Senator Oluremi Tinubu - Hon. Omobolanle Akinyemiobe; Prof. Remi Sonaya; HR Executive MTN Nigeria Communications Limited,Mrs Amina Oyagbola; Co-ordinator, DFID South-West, Dr Adesina Fagbenro; and Public Affairs Officer, US Consulate, Katy Bondy.

Grab your copy of Abiola Salami's best-selling book

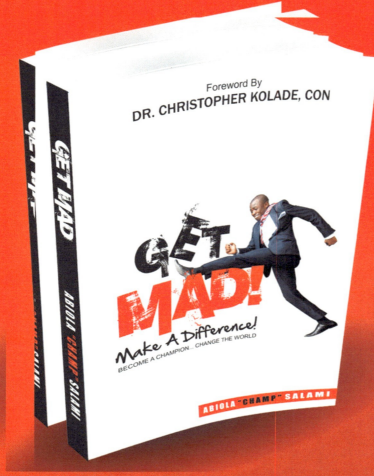

Get MAD!

Get MAD! is Abiola Champ Salami's brand new inspirational book. Drawing examples from several real life situations and true personal stories, Get MAD! is a call to be a Champion by making the necessary positive changes in our personal, corporate and communal lives.

Abiola's approach of Get MAD! is a call for this generation to make a positive difference; his thinking is that the disconnect between our abundant resources and the standard of living of our people should shock us into doing something out of the ordinary. – Dr. Christopher Kolade, CON, Nigeria's foremost elder statesman

Get MAD! is available in e-book, soft cover and hardcover format. You can order copies of Get MAD! from Ingram, Amazon.com; Barnes & Noble; Authorhouse online bookstore and local bookstores around you.

Available online on:

I Am A CHAMP is produced by Abiola "Champ" Salami as an innovative solution which thousands of people across the globe have described have described as a mind-blowing self-affirmative tonic helping them in discovering, developing and retaining their identity as champions in the face of challenges and other realities of life.

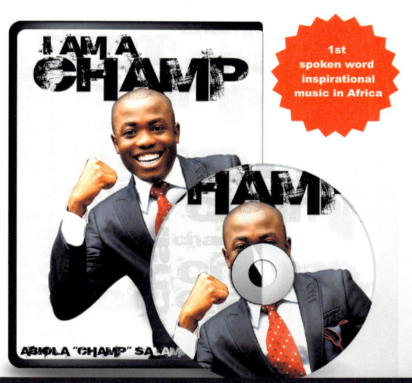

1st spoken word inspirational music in Africa

I Am A Champ Callertunes

MTN
035463   Keep keeping on
004399   Be Happy
004400   Push

Download Instruction:
Send tunecode to 4100 e.g. to buy PUSH, send 004400 to 4100.

AIRTEL
0086213   I am a Champ
0086214   Keep keeping on
0086212   Be Happy
0086215   Push

Download instruction:
To download PUSH. send BUY 0086215 to 791, please note the space between BUY and the code,

GLOBACOM
033517   I am a Champ
033518   Keep keeping on
033516   Be Happy
033519   Push

Download Instruction:
Send REG to 7728 to register. Then, send tune with Tune code to 7728 e.g. to buy BE HAPPY, send tune033516 to 7728. (Kindly note that there is no space between the tune and the code.

ETISALAT
88813451   I am a Champ
88813452   Keep keeping on
88813450   Be Happy
88813453   Push

Download Instruction:
Send the tune code to 251, e.g to download I AM CHAMP, send "download88813451" as a text message to 251.

Printed in the United States
By Bookmasters